D1062644

Out & About in Singapore

Text by **Melanie Lee**
Illustrations by **William Sim**

 **Marshall Cavendish**
Editions

© 2020 Marshall Cavendish International (Asia) Private Limited

Reprinted 2021

Published by Marshall Cavendish Editions
An imprint of Marshall Cavendish International

A member of the
Times Publishing Group

All rights reserved

No part of this publication may be reproduced, stored in a retrieval system or transmitted,
in any form or by any means, electronic, mechanical, photocopying, recording or otherwise,
without the prior permission of the copyright owner. Requests for permissions should be
addressed to the Publisher, Marshall Cavendish International (Asia) Private Limited,
1 New Industrial Road, Singapore 536196. Tel: (65) 6213 9300.
E-mail: genref@sg.marshallcavendish.com Website: www.marshallcavendish.com

The publisher makes no representation or warranties with respect to the contents of this book,
and specifically disclaims any implied warranties or merchantability or fitness for any particular
purpose, and shall in no event be liable for any loss of profit or any other commercial damage,
including but not limited to special, incidental, consequential, or other damages.

Other Marshall Cavendish Offices:
Marshall Cavendish Corporation, 800 Westchester Ave, Suite N-641, Rye Brook,
NY 10573, USA • Marshall Cavendish International (Thailand) Co Ltd, 253 Asoke,
16th Floor, Sukhumvit 21 Road, Klongtoey Nua, Wattana, Bangkok 10110, Thailand •
Marshall Cavendish (Malaysia) Sdn Bhd, Times Subang, Lot 46, Subang Hi-Tech
Industrial Park, Batu Tiga, 40000 Shah Alam, Selangor Darul Ehsan, Malaysia

Marshall Cavendish is a registered trademark of Times Publishing Limited

National Library Board, Singapore Cataloguing in Publication Data

Name(s): Lee, Melanie, 1979-. | Sim, William, 1967-, illustrator.
Title: Out & about in Singapore / text by Melanie Lee ; illustrations by William Sim.
Description: Singapore : Marshall Cavendish Editions, 2020.
Identifier(s): OCN 1124640657 | ISBN 978-981-4841-55-9
Subject(s): LCSH: Singapore—Description and travel—Juvenile literature. |
Singapore—History—Juvenile literature.
Classification: DDC 915.95704—dc23

Printed in Singapore

CONTENTS

INTRODUCTION

WELCOME TO SINGAPORE!

We're a small country located in Southeast Asia. Despite our size, there is a lot of fun stuff to do in Singapore . From futuristic buildings to beautiful gardens, there's something for everyone!

The world's tallest indoor waterfall greets you at Jewel Changi Airport.

FULL OF FLATS

If you ever come to Singapore, the first thing you'll notice are the many colourful high-rise buildings. These are called HDB (Housing Development Board) flats, and over 80% of Singapore's population live in these flats.

SMALLISH SINGAPORE

Just how small is Singapore? It has an area of 719 square kilometres. This is about half the size of Bangkok or London, or two-thirds the size of Hong Kong.

Despite her size, around six million people live in Singapore, making it a vibrant and bustling city!

CITY IN A GARDEN

Singapore may have many tall buildings, but there's also plenty of greenery. Our roads are lined with trees and flowering bushes, and there are also nature reserves and parks. These not only beautify Singapore, they also protect the environment and the rich variety of living things in the country.

HISTORY

HOT TRADING SPOT

Singapore has been a popular trading spot since the 13th century. Back then, it was called Temasek. Singapore is located between major trading routes and possesses a natural deep-water harbour. As such, even way back then, traders came from all over the world to buy and sell cloth, spices and porcelain here.

HOW SINGAPORE GOT ITS NAME

Many children in Singapore are told this local folktale by their parents and teachers:

In the 13th century, a Sumatran prince called Sang Nila Utama was hunting in the nearby island of Bintan and chased a stag up a hill. He couldn't find the stag when he reached the top of the hill, but saw an island with a white sandy beach. His men told him that the island was called Temasek.

He decided to visit the island, but his ship was caught in a storm while travelling there. He and his men threw out all their heavy things, but water kept entering the ship. The captain advised him to throw his crown overboard as a gift to the sea. Once the prince did that, the storm died down and he reached the island safely.

While hunting on this island, he saw an animal with a red body, a black head and a white breast. His chief minister told him that it was a lion. Sang Nila Utama took this to be a good omen and decided to build his new city here. He renamed it Singapura, which means "lion city" in Sanskrit.

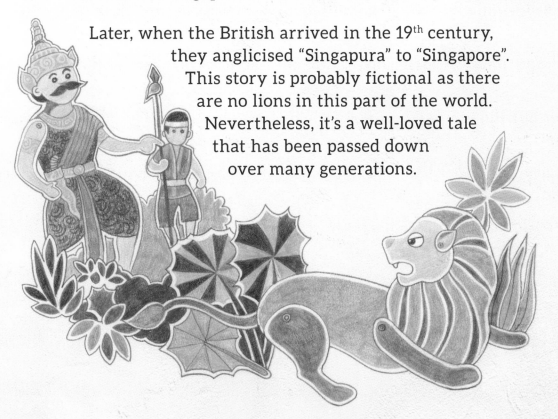

Later, when the British arrived in the 19th century, they anglicised "Singapura" to "Singapore". This story is probably fictional as there are no lions in this part of the world. Nevertheless, it's a well-loved tale that has been passed down over many generations.

A BRITISH COLONY

In 1819, Sir Stamford Raffles of the British East India Company arrived in Singapore and decided that it would make an ideal British trading post for the trade route between Asia and Europe. The British also set up plantations growing nutmeg and rubber here. After that, many migrants from China and India came here to seek their fortunes.

Singapore became a British colony in 1824 and remained one until 1963. Until today, English is the main language of this country.

SINGAPORE'S INDEPENDENCE

Between 1963 and 1965, Singapore was a part of Malaysia. However, because Singapore was so different from the rest of Malaysia, it was decided that it would be better for Singapore to become an independent nation.

Even though Singapore is a young and small country without any natural resources, it has grown to become one of the most developed countries in Southeast Asia.

THE CIVIC DISTRICT

The Civic District is a great starting point in discovering Singapore's history and heritage. Here, you will come across museums, art venues, as well as heritage architecture that reveal the fascinating culture and history of this country.

THE SINGAPORE RIVER: WHERE IT ALL BEGAN

When Singapore became a British trading centre in 1819, the Singapore River was abuzz with activity as new migrants set up businesses and homes around this area.

Today, it is no longer a harbour, but it continues to be a popular major landmark in Singapore with restaurants, cafes, hotels and museums lined along the river bank at the Civic District.

THE BIG CLEAN-UP!

In the 1970s, the Singapore River was polluted and full of rubbish. The government took ten years to clean up the river from 1977 to 1987. Squatters were relocated to HDB flats while street hawkers were shifted to hawker centres. Today, it is a lovely scenic area perfect for a stroll or a jog!

INTERESTING FIGURES

Look out for these larger-than-life statues when you're strolling along the Singapore River!

This statue of Sir Stamford Raffles is located at Empress Place. It marks the spot where he first landed in Singapore. Raffles is regarded as the founder of modern Singapore.

First Generation by artist Chong Fah Chong recreates a common olden-day scene of young boys leaping into the river. This work is located in front of The Fullerton Hotel.

The River Merchants by artist Aw Tee Hong depicts people interacting and working during a typical work day in the early 19th century. This work is located in front of Maybank Tower.

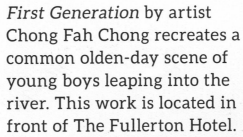

EXPERIENCING SINGAPORE'S STORY

The **National Museum of Singapore** was built in 1887 and is the country's oldest museum. Its interactive galleries bring Singapore's history to life from the 14th century right to the present day. Here, you can view interesting artefacts such as Chinese gold jewellery, coins and pottery found from archaeological digs.

HOT ROMANTIC SPOT

The museum still retains its elegant colonial architecture since it is a National Monument. As such, many couples choose to take their wedding photos here as it is very beautiful.

HOME OF MODERN ART

The **National Gallery Singapore** houses over 8,000 pieces of art from Singapore and Southeast Asia from the 19th century to the present day. The gallery's architecture itself is a work of art. Formerly the City Hall and Supreme Court buildings, they have been beautifully restored and creatively adapted to function as a major art museum.

ART JUST FOR KIDS

The National Gallery Singapore makes art fun for kids! Besides holding regular storytelling sessions to help young visitors appreciate art, the Keppel Centre for Art Education lets children, youths and families immerse themselves in art in a playful manner.

AN ARTS HAVEN

There's always something happening at **Esplanade – Theatres on the Bay**, Singapore's national performing arts centre. Over 3,000 performances take place every year, and many of them are free so that everyone can enjoy the arts!

INSPIRED BY SINGAPORE'S FAVOURITE FRUIT

The nickname for Esplanade is "durian" because of its resemblance to the spiky and thorny Southeast Asian "king of fruits" which is well-loved by many Singaporeans. Its two spiky domes house the Concert Hall and Theatre.

DARE TO DURIAN?

The durian not only looks scary, its taste and smell is pretty intense as well! Like blue cheese, people either love it or hate it. Durian lovers adore its creamy custard texture and savoury sweet taste. Those who hate it say that it smells like rotten eggs and tastes bitter. During durian season (usually in August and September), durian-loving Singaporeans get together with friends and family to enjoy this fruit.

HOUSES OF WORSHIP

Given that the Civic District was where the British first started
building Singapore up, you will find many old European-style
churches here. These are two that we find pretty charming.

THE RED BRICK CHURCH

Prinsep Street Presbyterian Church is Singapore's oldest
Presbyterian church. It was set up in 1837 by a British
missionary. The current building was completed in 1931
in a modern fresco style inspired by Spanish architecture.

THE NEO-GOTHIC CHURCH

St. Andrew's Cathedral is the oldest Anglican church in Singapore. It was built in 1864 by Indian convict labourers. Before this cathedral, the site had a church built in 1838. However, it had to be demolished due to damage from lightning strikes. Today, St. Andrew's is one of the few remaining buildings in Singapore built in an English neo-Gothic style.

CHINATOWN

Chinatown is an area steeped in rich history. In the
19th century, it was a bustling place where many early
Chinese immigrants lived and worked. As such, you can
still spot many heritage buildings here!

CHINATOWN'S NICKNAME

Many Singaporeans also refer to
Chinatown here as *Niu Che Shui* which
means "bullock cart water" in Mandarin.
This name came from the fact that
the bullock cart was a popular form of
transportation in the 19th century. Clean
water was also high in demand back
then, and some enterprising merchants
would sell and deliver clean water
around Chinatown in bullock carts.

THIAN HOCK KENG TEMPLE

Enter Singapore's oldest Chinese temple to appreciate its intricate carvings and majestic structures. Thian Hock Keng Temple was built in 1840 by early Chinese immigrants to thank Mazu, the goddess of the sea, for their safe voyage from China to Singapore. Did you know that this temple once faced the sea? However, because of land reclamation, this temple is now surrounded by shophouses.

CHINATOWN FOOD STREET

Looking for a spot where you can sample all of Singapore's world famous street food? Chinatown Food Street (on Smith Street) has 24 street hawker stalls and six restaurants with plenty to offer in terms of local treats. We recommend the *Bak Kut Teh*, which means "meat bone tea" in Hokkien, and Chicken Rice, which is always a favourite with kids!

LUNAR NEW YEAR

When the Lunar New Year approaches (usually around January or February), Chinatown blossoms into a bustling area as people come here to shop for clothes, food and decorations to celebrate the festival. The streets are lined with beautiful lanterns, and there are colourful processions and lion dances to make Chinatown even more festive.

HOW TO MAKE A CHINESE LANTERN

MATERIALS & TOOLS

- 1 piece of red construction paper
- 1 empty toilet roll
- Red paint
- 1 metre of twine
- 1 stick
- Pencil
- Ruler
- Scissors
- Paintbrush
- Glue
- Stapler

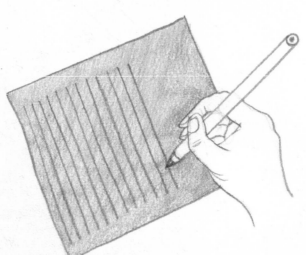

1. Draw horizontal lines along the red construction paper, leaving a 1 cm gap between each line. Also leave a border around the edges of the paper.

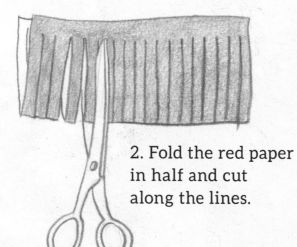

2. Fold the red paper in half and cut along the lines.

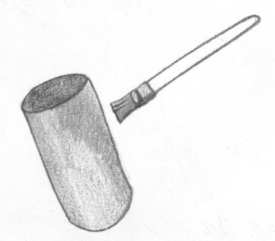

3. Paint the toilet roll red and let the paint dry.

4. After the paint has dried, glue the red construction paper on the toilet roll in such a way that the red paper bulges out.

5. Divide the twine into three parts. Tie a knot on each end of the twine and staple it inside the lantern on opposing sides. Gather the other end of the twines and tie to one end of the stick.

6. Your lantern is ready!

KAMPONG GLAM

A BLEND OF OLD AND NEW

Kampong Glam was set aside as the Muslim enclave of Singapore in the early 19th century. "Kampong" means village in Malay while "Glam" comes from the cajeput (known in Malay as *Gelam*) trees that used to grow here. Up till today, there's a strong traditional Malay-Arab influence in this area. At the same time, some parts of Kampong Glam are also pretty hip with cafes, bars, vintage shops and colourful wall art. It definitely makes for an interesting visit!

THE SULTAN MOSQUE

The most famous landmark at Kampong Glam is the Sultan Mosque with its majestic golden dome and impressive prayer hall that can hold up to 5,000 people. Opt for a guided tour to find out more about the history of this building and the Islamic faith.

AN OLD PALACE

Malay royalty once stayed at this elegant compound known as the **Istana Kampong Glam**. Today, the former palace is home to the Malay Heritage Centre where you can learn more about the heritage and culture of Singapore's Malay community.

CELEBRATING HARI RAYA PUASA

Hari Raya Puasa marks the end of a month of fasting for Muslims. Fasting is seen as a way to purify the heart and the mind. During this month of fasting known as Ramadan, there will be a night street bazaar selling plenty of delicious Malay snacks and food around Sultan Mosque for those who break their fast after sunset.

A DIFFERENT TYPE OF SHOPPING

Explore the diverse mix of little shops nestled in shophouses along the narrow alleyways of Kampong Glam. We really like the multi-generational family businesses selling carpets, textiles and perfumes. In such places, you probably can pick up things that you'll never find in the usual shopping malls!

KETUPAT CRAFT

A popular festive food is the *ketupat*, a compressed rice dumpling wrapped in woven coconut leaves. It is usually eaten with meat or stews.

Here's how you can make your very own ketupat decoration.

1. Draw horizontal lines along one of the papers, leaving a 1 cm gap between each line Also leave a border around the edges of the paper.

MATERIALS & TOOLS

• Two pieces of square paper of different colours, preferably yellow and green

• Pencil

• Glue

• Scissors

• Ribbons

• Stapler

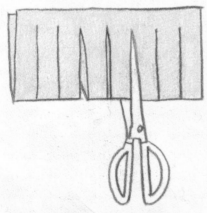

2. Fold the paper in half and cut along the lines.

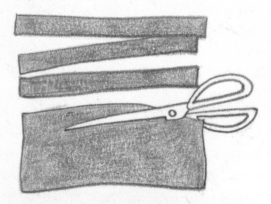

3. Cut out 1 – 2 cm strips from the other piece of paper.

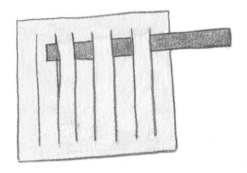

4. Take one paper strip and weave it over and under the slits.

5. Take another strip and weave it in an opposite pattern i.e. under and over the slits.

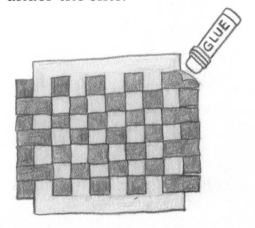

6. Glue the strips in place.

7. Place the woven square papers as a diamond and staple a ribbon loop at the top and glue on ribbon strips at the bottom.

LITTLE INDIA

Little India is a lively neighbourhood which forms the heart of Singapore's South Asian community. Here, you will find a colourful range of shops selling spices, sarees and jewellery, as well as restaurants, trendy cafes and hostels.

SHOP AROUND THE CLOCK

If you love great deals and countless options when shopping – you have to visit Mustafa Centre. This 24-hour department store sells practically everything under the sun from toys and clothes to fruits and electronics on its six levels.

SRI VEERAMAKALIAMMAN TEMPLE

This is one of the oldest Hindu temples in Singapore and is best known for its intricate, colourful statues of deities carved on its gopuram. The gopuram is the entrance gateway to the temple. Built in 1855 by Indian labourers, the temple is dedicated to the Goddess Kali, the destroyer of evil.

POWER BREAKFAST

Little India is the best place to find spicy food. In particular, Roti Prata is very popular amongst Singaporeans as a breakfast dish. Roti Prata looks like a crispy pancake, and it is typically dipped into curry gravy. This dish is often accompanied by a cup of *Teh Tarik* ("tarik" means "pull" in Malay), which is pulled black tea with condensed milk. The tea is "pulled" by pouring it from a height into another cup to cool it down and improve its flavour.

FESTIVAL OF LIGHTS

During the Deepavali season (usually in November), Little India is aglow with light decorations as Hindus, Sikhs and some Buddhists celebrate the triumph of good over evil. Bazaars are set up where devotees can buy floral garlands, incense and traditional snacks while getting their henna tattoos done.

A DEEPAVALI CANDLE HOLDER

Since Deepavali is all about how light triumphs over darkness in this world, here's a craft you can make to bring more light to your home!

MATERIALS & TOOLS

- Air-dry clay of assorted colours

- Water

- White glue

- Craft gems, beads and other decorations

- Tealight candle

1. Shape a candle holder from air-dry clay. Ensure it is big enough for a tealight candle to fit in. Wet your finger and press gently to smooth out any cracks. Let it dry.

2. Create decorations from the clay such as flowers and stars. Let them dry.

3. Glue the clay decorations, along with the gems and beads to the holder.

4. Place the candle into the middle. Get your parents to help you light the candle and enjoy!

JOO CHIAT

DISCOVER PERANAKAN CULTURE

"Peranakan" means "locally born" in Malay. Many Peranakans (who usually have a mixed Chinese and Malay/Indonesian heritage) live in Joo Chiat. This unique culture is known for its vibrant colours – something you're sure to notice when you visit this charming neighbourhood full of shops, restaurants and cafes.

PRETTY PASTEL SHOPHOUSES

In Joo Chiat, there is a special street called Koon Seng Road that is lined with restored 1920s and 1930s conserved shophouses. They have been painted in pastel colours and are adorned with intricately decorated Peranakan tiles. Many locals and tourists flock here to take photographs of themselves in front of these lovely buildings.

ALL THINGS PERANAKAN AT THE INTAN

If you're curious to find out more about Peranakan culture, make an appointment to visit The Intan. This private home-museum houses over 1,500 vintage Peranakan artefacts including enamel tiffin carriers and beaded shoes. The owner, Alvin Yapp, has travelled around the world collecting these items to showcase Peranakan heritage.

MARINA BAY SANDS

TOP OF THE WORLD

Marina Bay Sands is Singapore's most famous building with its unique boat-shaped rooftop. Besides housing a hotel, casino, theatre, museum, restaurants and shops, it also has majestic 360-degree views of Singapore from the 57th floor. If you are a hotel guest, you could even take in this breathtaking scenery from its rooftop Infinity Pool, which is the largest pool of its kind in the world.

ARTSCIENCE MUSEUM

You might be wondering, what is inside this mysterious lotus-inspired building next to Marina Bay Sands? This is the ArtScience Museum, which partners with the most renowned galleries and museums in the world to present cutting edge exhibitions on art, science and culture. Do check out its permanent exhibition, "Future World", which is a dazzling display of interactive digital installations.

LIGHT & WATER SHOW

Every night, Marina Bay Sands puts up a magical outdoor light and water show called "Spectra" at its Event Plaza which is along the Singapore River. It is a stunning, high-tech symphony of colourful laser lights, dancing water fountains, visual arts and orchestral music that tells the story of Singapore's past, present and future.

SINGAPORE BOTANIC GARDENS

GARDENS WITH A HISTORY

The Singapore Botanic Gardens is a UNESCO World Heritage site. It was built in 1859 by the British as a place to collect, grow and experiment with plants that could be useful in this region. Today, the 82-hectare Gardens houses over 10,000 species of flora and is a popular nature spot for both locals and tourists alike.

RUBBER CONNECTION

The Gardens' first Director, Sir Henry Nicholas Ridley, helped to develop the rubber industry through his research. In the late 19th century, the English botanist looked into ways to tap rubber latex without harming the trees, and how latex could be prepared for sale.

GORGEOUS GREENERY

There's much of nature's beauty to take in when you visit the Gardens. For a start, you can go on the Rain Forest walking trail to walk through some of the oldest rainforests in Singapore. As the Gardens has been around for so long, you will also find a few majestic old trees amidst the lush greenery. Look out for the 200-year-old Tembusu Tree which grandly stands around 30 metres tall.

JACOB BALLAS CHILDREN'S GARDEN

The Singapore Botanic Gardens also houses the largest children's garden in Asia with the Jacob Ballas Children's Garden (for kids up to 14 years old). It's a great space to explore with a Tree House playground, a suspension bridge, a maze and much more.

NATIONAL ORCHID GARDEN

Here is where you can find the world's largest collection of orchids with over 600 varieties. There is also a special collection of orchids named after celebrities and foreign dignitaries who have visited the Gardens over the years.

VANDA MISS JOAQUIM

Meet Singapore's national flower at the Singapore Botanic Gardens. Vanda Miss Joaquim is a hybrid between the *Vanda hookeriana* and *Vanda teres* orchids. It was first bred by Singapore-born Armenian, Agnes Joaquim, in her garden around 1893. The flower is known for its beauty and hardiness.

GARDENS BY THE BAY

SUPER DUPER SUPERTREES

You know you're in a very special park when you first see the futuristic Supertrees at Gardens by the Bay. These 18 Supertrees are made out of steel and concrete, and measure between 25 and 50 metres tall. They provide shade and are also home to around 163,000 plants.

FLOWER POWER

The Flower Dome is the largest greenhouse in Singapore and over 3,300 glass panels were used to build it! The interior is kept cool and dry like a Mediterranean climate.

COOL OFF!

At the Far East Organisation Children's Garden there's a water play area for some splashing good fun (don't forget your swimming costume). Even the sprinklers here are futuristic. They come with sensors to detect your movements which can then create different fun water effects in response!

CLOUD HIGH

Enter the misty Cloud Forest and discover the rich biodiversity of plants in the tropical highlands. You will also find the world's second tallest indoor waterfall nestled within the lush greenery of this dome. Take a stroll on the Cloud Walk platform for the best bird's eye view of this conservatory.

MARINA BARRAGE

A SPECIAL RESERVOIR

The Marina Barrage is Singapore's 15th reservoir and provides up to 10% of the local water supply. It has flood prevention features with release gates and pumps that channel excess water to the sea during the rainy season. Perhaps what is most special about this place is its unusual design that makes it a popular recreational spot.

LET'S GO FLY A KITE

The Marina Barrage has a spacious roof garden that receives winds from the shorelines. This makes it an ideal spot for kite flying, especially with the scenic Singapore skyline as a backdrop. During the weekends, many people come here for picnics because of the breeze and the view.

FUN IN THE SUN

Besides kite flying, you can also rent a kayak or canoe to paddle on the calm reservoir waters. If you just want to splash about, there's the Marina Barrage Water Playground with fountains and water jets.

SAVING THE ENVIRONMENT

Having a clean and green environment is important to many Singaporeans. The Marina Barrage is environmentally friendly. At the Sustainable Singapore Gallery, you can find out more about what Singapore is doing to overcome environmental challenges and promote a sustainable lifestyle nationwide. You can also visit The Solar Park, which has over 400 panels that provide electricity needed for lighting the barrage.

LEE KONG CHIAN
NATURAL HISTORY MUSEUM

Located at the National University of Singapore, the Lee Kong Chian Natural History Museum is Southeast Asia's first natural history museum. It is a haven for nature lovers who hope to find out more about the rich variety of plants and animals in Southeast Asia.

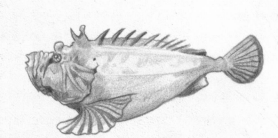

LIFE ON EARTH

The Biodiversity Gallery on the first floor is divided into 15 zones according to the types of plant and animals as well as other scientific themes. There are a few thousand specimens and replicas on display and the sheer variety in shape, colour, and size is astounding!

GIANT FOSSILS

Perhaps the most impressive exhibits here would be the three dinosaurs named Prince, Apollonia and Twinky. These fossils are 27m, 24m and 12m long respectively, and are considered among the largest animals to have walked on land. Each of them is about 80% complete — a rarity in the dinosaur fossil world. You can also see the Singapore Sperm Whale (measuring 10.6m) that is displayed in a diving pose. In 2015, its body was found floating off Jurong Island and the museum worked to salvage this specimen.

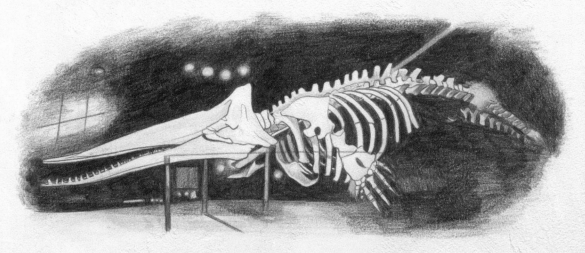

HAW PAR VILLA

A ONE-OF-A-KIND ASIAN CULTURAL PARK

If you're looking for a spot in Singapore to get the quirkiest photographs your friends will all be envious of, Haw Par Villa is the place to go. This zany theme park in the western part of Singapore presents Asian culture, history, philosophy and religion in a fun way with giant and colourful displays and statues.

THE TIGER BALM CONNECTION

Haw Par Villa used to be called Tiger Balm Garden. It was built in 1937 by Aw Boon Haw, the creator of Tiger Balm (a popular medical ointment). By opening the park to the public, Aw hoped that its portrayal of Asian mythology and values would guide visitors on what is right and wrong and become better people.

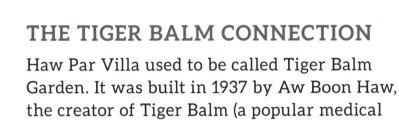

TEN COURTS OF HELL

Many classic Chinese folktales are presented at Haw Par Villa, but perhaps its most famous exhibit would be the Ten Courts of Hell. It is a 60-metre-long trail depicting different courts of hell and the punishments meted out depending on the evil deeds being committed. Some Singaporean parents bring their children to see this attraction to encourage them to behave.

NIGHT SAFARI

INTO THE WILD

When the sun sets, make your way to the north of Singapore where you will find the Night Safari, the world's first nocturnal safari park housed in a dense rainforest. This unique attraction brings you up close with over 900 animals, many of which are endangered in this region.

STARS FOR THE NIGHT

A trip to the Night Safari has to include watching the Creatures of the Night Show. Here, you'll be introduced to some of the cutest and cleverest nocturnal creatures such as the binturongs, otters, civets and owls.

TRAM IT

A most relaxing way to explore the park is to hop on the tram. The 40-minute ride includes a guide providing live commentary on the various animals you will encounter. The tram will take you on a journey through seven geographical zones: Himalayan Foothills, Indian Subcontinent, Equatorial Africa, Indo-Malayan Region, Asian Riverine Forest, Nepalese River Valley and Burmese Hillside.

PULAU UBIN

AN ISLAND GETAWAY

Singapore has a few surrounding islands worth exploring. One of them is Pulau Ubin, which is a ten-minute boat ride from Changi Jetty. Its name comes from its original Malay name, Pulau Batu Jubin, which means "Island of Granite Stones".

If you've ever wondered what Singapore was like before it became a bustling city full of towering buildings, exploring rustic Pulau Ubin will give you a good idea. Look out for the traditional *kampongs* (villages), coconut and rubber plantations, and farms!

NATURE WONDERLAND

A must-see spot at Pulau Ubin is Chek Jawa Wetlands. This unique 100-hectare pocket of nature supports six ecosystems: sandy beach, rocky beach, seagrass lagoon, coral rubble, mangroves and coastal forest. During low tide, you can see how the area is teeming with rich plant and marine life from the boardwalk. There's also a viewing tower for bird-watching.

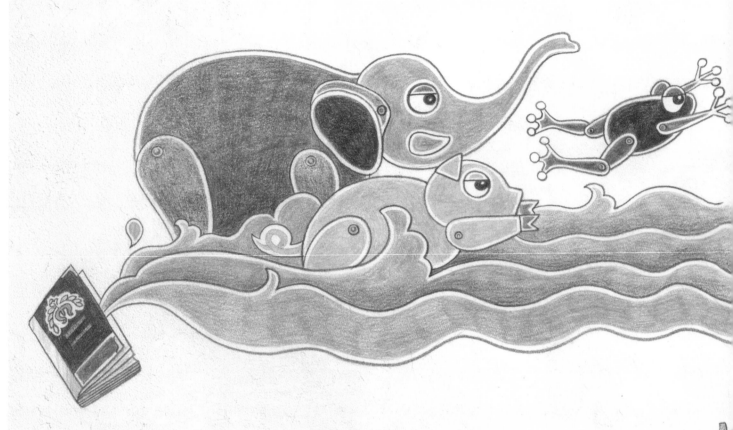

THE PIG, THE ELEPHANT & THE FROG

A popular folktale about Pulau Ubin revolves around a pig, an elephant and a frog who challenged each other to swim from Singapore to Johor, Malaysia. Whoever did not reach the finishing line would be turned to rock.

The swim across the Straits of Johor proved far more challenging and none of them made it across. The frog, who first attempted this feat, did not make it across and eventually formed an islet known as Pulau Sekudu ("Frog Island" in Malay). The elephant and pig had their turns but failed as well, and both of them fused together to become the island of Pulau Ubin.

CYCLING AROUND UBIN

The best way to get around Pulau Ubin is by cycling. When you reach the island, you will see many bicycle stalls where you can rent a bicycle of your liking. Cycling allows you to explore more of the island, and at a leisurely pace that lets you take in the sights of this idyllic place.

SENTOSA

ISLAND ADVENTURE

There are many fun things to do on the resort island of Sentosa — beaches, theme parks, nature trails and so much more! There are countless entertainment options both indoors and outdoors. You can stay at any of the hotels and resorts within the island for a few days to soak in all that adventure. The most charming way to get to Sentosa is by Cable Car, where you'll get a scenic view of the sea and the city.

FORT SILOSO: PROTECTING SINGAPORE

The British decided to build four forts in Sentosa to protect Singapore's harbour from invasion by sea. Of these, only one remains today – Fort Siloso. It is an interesting historical site where you can still see coastal guns and the remains of military structures and tunnels.

A PIRATE HIDEOUT

Before Sentosa was called Sentosa (which means "peace and tranquillity" in Malay) in 1972, this island used to be called Pulau Blakang Mati (which means "island behind death"). It was apparently given this name because of the pirates who would pillage boats passing by the island between the 15th and 19th centuries.

This waterway between mainland Singapore and Sentosa was known by sailors to be particularly dangerous, and the pirates were known to attack with blowguns and slaughter their victims.

KUSU ISLAND

THE TURTLE-SHAPED ISLAND

Kusu Island, which is around 5.6 kilometres from mainland Singapore, is shaped like a turtle and has been named as such. Kusu means "turtle" in Hokkien. It's the perfect spot for a picnic with its lagoons and pristine beaches. You can also explore the rich living coral of this island during low tide and perhaps even spot a sea turtle or two! To get to Kusu Island, take a ferry from Marina South Pier.

TURTLE POWER

Legend has it that during a rough storm, two shipwrecked fishermen (one Malay and one Chinese) stranded at sea were rescued by a giant magical turtle who turned into an island so they could swim ashore. Later, the fishermen built a Chinese temple and a Malay shrine on the island in gratitude to the mysterious creature who saved them from drowning.

A SPIRITUAL PILGRIMAGE

There are three Malay shrines and a Chinese temple on Kusu Island. Every year, on the ninth month of the lunar calendar (around October/November), devotees will make their way to Kusu Island to pay their respects to the God of Prosperity (or "Tua Pek Kong" in Hokkien) and the Goddess of Mercy (or "Kuan Yin" in Hokkien). People pray to these temple deities for longevity, wealth and peace. Devotees looking for specific blessings in marriage, fertility, health or harmony will climb 152 steps to reach the three shrines of Malay saints and pay their respects.

SPEAKING LIKE A SINGAPOREAN

In Singapore, locals speak a language known as Singlish, which is a mixture of English, Malay, Tamil and a few Chinese dialects. It might initially sound confusing, but knowing these few common Singlish terms might help you connect with a friendly Singaporean!

LAH

Meaning: A term usually used at the end of a sentence for emphasis.

Example: I don't know *lah*.

CAN

Meaning: A term that usually means no problem.

Example: Can you show me how to get to Marina Bay Sands? *Can*.

ALAMAK

Meaning: An expression of dismay, surprise or alarm.

Example: *Alamak*! Why is it so hot today?

MAKAN

Meaning: Usually refers to having a meal or eating.

Example: Let's go *makan* in Chinatown!

CHOPE

Meaning: To reserve a place or an item.

Example: Can you *chope* this table for us while we buy food?

SHIOK

Meaning: To express great satisfaction.

Example: The foot massage I went for is *shiok*! I feel so relaxed now.

ONZ

Meaning: To express an acknowledgement of an appointment or agreement.

Example: Can we meet at Esplanade tonight? *Onz*! See you there.

FAREWELL NOTE

Dear reader,

We hope that you have had fun exploring Singapore through this book!

If you live in Singapore, we hope that you have learned some interesting things about this country and discovered new places to visit.

If you're on a holiday here, we hope that this book will give you some fun ideas on how to enjoy our sunny island with your family.

If anything, we hope that this book has shown you that our country has something for everybody, despite its humble size. Have fun going out and about in Singapore in real life!

Your fellow Singapore explorers,

Melanie & William

MAP OF SINGAPORE

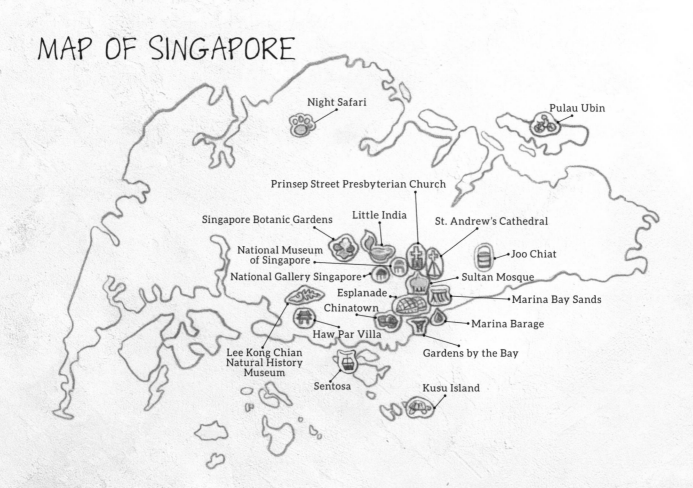